MINUTE MONOLOGUES *for* KIDS

Ruth Mae Roddy

Dramaline® Publications

Dramaline Publications
36-851 Palm View Road
Rancho Mirage, CA 92270
Phone 760/770-6076 Fax 760/770-4507
E-Mail: dramaline@aol.com
www.dramaline.com

Cover by John Sabel

This book is printed on 55# Glatfelter acid-free paper, a paper that meets the requirements of the American Standard of Permanence of paper for printed library material.

Minute Monologues for Kids

WORKSHEET

_____

_____

_____

_____

_____

_____

_____

_____

_____

_____

_____

_____

THE VISIT

Family road-trips are often less than fun.

Every Christmas we go to Aunt Florence's house. It's way over on the other side of the state. Takes us forever. I gotta sit in the back seat of our car with Harold and Freddy–my two weird brothers. They torment me all the way. Really bug me, you know.

Usually it's snowing or raining or something. Every time. Never nice and sunny. One time we broke down in this little town where people looked like outer space. My mom called it The Twilight Zone. It was scary. We had lunch in this diner where people stared at us all the time, didn't take their eyes off us. Like we were some kind of crazy, or something. One man didn't have any teeth, just gums. I couldn't figure out how he ate.

Looks like we're in for it again this year, too. We gotta drag a whole bunch of stuff to Aunt Florence's. Plus Harold wants to take the cat. I'm sure glad Merry Christmas comes only once a year.

WORKSHEET

_____

_____

_____

_____

_____

_____

_____

_____

_____

_____

_____

_____

NEIGHBORS

Good neighbors come in all sizes.

There's this man next door who throws garbage in our yard. Mr. Gambrini. My dad comes unglued when he does this and has talked to him about it lots of times, but he still keeps tossing junk over the fence.

Mr. Gambrini is eighty-five years old. His wife died last year, and he lives alone with a bunch of ugly dogs. My mom feels sorry for him, but my dad thinks he's nuts. Sometimes we hear him singing songs that my mother says are Italian. I don't understand them, but they still sound kinda neat.

Today when my dad got home from work he found a Coke can in our yard. He blew up big and was just about to go over and yell at Mr. Gambrini when he shows up at our front door with a present for Mom. It was this really neat silk scarf that used to belong to his wife. Said it was her favorite and he wanted Mom to have it. His hands were real shaky.

My dad didn't yell at him. How can you yell at someone like that?

WORKSHEET

_____

_____

_____

_____

_____

_____

_____

_____

_____

_____

_____

_____

BIG IDEAS

We can't have everything we see.

I love surfing the Net. It's kinda like looking in on the whole world, or something. Every time I open it up, I'm totally amazed at all the stuff that's there.

I found this one site where you can find out all about cars: how much they cost, how powerful they are–everything. My favorite is the new Jaguar. Boy, you talk about cool.

When I mentioned to my dad that we should trade for a new Jaguar, he looked at me like I was crazy. He goes, "And just where you think I'm gonna get that kind of money?" Why is it grownups all the time think about nothing but money? I mean, what's money have to do with wanting to be seen driving around in a new Jaguar instead of a beat-up Jeep Cherokee?

Dad said maybe I shouldn't spend so much time on the computer, that maybe it's giving me crazy ideas. Hey! What's so crazy about wanting a cool ride?

WORKSHEET

CHRISTMAS WISH

'Tis the night before school starts, and I'm so down
in the dumps,
I think about faking a case of the mumps.
My backpack's so full of books and supplies,
That I can't even lift it without bugging my eyes.
My sister is calling her friends on the cell,
All, "I can't wait for tomorrow," she's crazy as . . .
well!
My mom's in her SUV, on her way to the mall,
To buy me some new clothes to wear for the fall,
That will look dumb and won't fit, but that doesn't
matter,
'Cause she just doesn't care if they make me look
fatter.
So away to my room I fly in a hurry
To turn on my computer and surf in a flurry,
For anything neat, for anything cool,
To take my mind off returning to school.

WORKSHEET

LOOKS

It's what's on the inside that counts.

We have this man in the neighborhood who's real funny looking. Us kids go out of our way to walk past his place to see if he's in his yard. He looks just like this toad in this book I have called *The Wind in the Willows.*

My dad says it's not polite to make fun of people, that me and my friends shouldn't do such stuff. Says that the way a person treats people and how he behaves is more important than how a person looks. And, you know what, he's right, 'cause yesterday, when we walked by the toad's place, he smiled at us and said, "Hello." He was washing his car, a brand-new red Corvette. Really cool. He let us sit in it and answered our questions about how fast it would go and stuff. He was super nice.

And you know what? After a while, he didn't look so toady anymore.

WORKSHEET

_____

_____

_____

_____

_____

_____

_____

_____

_____

_____

_____

_____

THE VISITOR

Mother knows best.

A couple of days ago, my Uncle Bill shows up. He's my mom's brother. He had this woman with him who was real cool. Her name is Kathy. She wears nice styles and is a lot younger than Uncle Bill. My mom wasn't very friendly to her. Maybe it's because she has this tattoo of a snake on her arm. When I told Mom I thought she was cool, she didn't say anything, just kept on wiping finger marks off the kitchen cabinets.

Last night Uncle Bill took us all to dinner to this place in Ridgewood that had tablecloths and guys running around filling up glasses. He ordered me a shrimp cocktail. It was a lot better than anything they have at Chuck E. Cheese.

Uncle Bill and Kathy are moving to Las Vegas. She says it's her favorite place in the world. She said I could come visit. When I mentioned this to Mom, she said she didn't think it was a good idea. I guess she's afraid I'll get a tattoo.

WORKSHEET

MUSIC LESSON

It takes hard work to be good.

Last year I saw this black piano in the window of
Morelli's Music Store. It shined like a wet prune. As
soon as I saw it, I knew I wanted to play the piano. I
could just see myself playing neat stuff for people
and being real popular.

When I asked my mom and dad if I could have a
piano, they said okay, if I promised to practice every
day.

At first it was easy. But by the time I got to the
second method, it got really hard. And I had to
practice an hour a day no matter what. While my
friends were out messing around, I had to stay in and
practice. And it seemed like I never got any better. In
fact, I got worse. So, finally, they let me quit, and Mr.
Morelli took back the piano. Wow, what a relief.

Messing around is a whole lot better than music.
You don't have to practice to mess around.

WORKSHEET

_____

_____

_____

_____

_____

_____

_____

_____

_____

_____

_____

_____

POOR PEOPLE

It's important to be kind.

Yesterday I went with my mom and dad to the homeless shelter. I was surprised at how many people were there. You just don't think about stuff like this.

They had a big tent there. In the tent were cots with blankets and pillows and stuff. Mom said that all the stuff was donated, but there still wasn't enough to go around. This is the reason we went there, to take some old blankets and clothing. I gave this one man one of my dad's old jackets. He looked like he was a hundred years old. He was very grateful. He told me he once had good job, but he got laid off and couldn't find anything to do. Even though he looked tired and old, he was very kind and had nice eyes and a nice smile. I couldn't believe it when I found out he was only forty years old. My dad is the same age, but he looks healthy and young. When I mentioned this to my dad, he said it's easy to look young when you have hope. I think I understand.

WORKSHEET

_____

_____

_____

_____

_____

_____

_____

_____

_____

_____

_____

_____

BED TIME

Sometimes it's hard to obey the rules.

Sometimes I wonder if anything at all goes on after ten o'clock at night. The reason I wonder is that I've never been up past ten. Ever. Even on New Year's. My sister tells me that neat stuff goes on later, but I'm not sure because my sister tells me all kinds of crazy stuff just to get on my nerves. Once she told me that rabbits get in drainpipes and can eat your toes while you're taking a shower. She's such a dork.

My parents are real strict about me being in bed early. They say kids my age need lots of rest. Hey, what about older people? I think they're the ones who need rest. My mom and dad are always complaining about being beat, but I have all kinds of energy and never get tired. If you ask me, they should be the ones in bed early, and I should be up seeing what happens after ten o'clock.

WORKSHEET

_____

_____

_____

_____

_____

_____

_____

_____

_____

_____

_____

_____

MERRY CHRISTMAS

Parents are often hard to understand.

Yesterday, my mom and dad went over their Christmas card list. They do this every year to make changes and add people and take people off. It's really a weird thing. My dad goes, "What about Julia Adams? We haven't gotten a card from her in years." Mom goes, "But she's Aunt Flora's daughter." My dad goes, "So what, we haven't spoken to Flora since she didn't come to Ruth's funeral." They cut her off. Then my mom goes, "Does Freddie still live in Sarasota?" My dad goes, "Who cares about that drunk? Cut him off." And Mom goes, "That's an awful thing to say about your first cousin." My dad goes, "Okay, but don't send him one of the good ones." Mom goes, "I wonder if Edith Walters is still living?" Dad goes, "You'll know if the card comes back Address Unknown." They leave her on. This is the way it went the whole afternoon. This is nothing–you should hear them when they decorate the tree.

WORKSHEET

_____

_____

_____

_____

_____

_____

_____

_____

_____

_____

_____

_____

_____

SMART PET

People aren't as tough as they let on.

A few weeks ago I went out back, and there was this little kitten. He was scrawny to the point you could see his ribs. My dad said not to feed him because, if we did, we'd own a cat. But my mom said she just couldn't let a little kitten starve to death, so she fed him some leftover tuna.

Well, my dad was right, 'cause now we have a full-time cat. At first my dad was going to take him to the pound, but every time he got ready to take him, the cat would jump up in his lap and start licking his hand.

So anyway, now we have a cat who hangs around the back of our house and sleeps in this little bed my mom bought him. My dad named him Leonard because he said he reminds him of Uncle Leonard who has hair longer than cats' whiskers growing out of his nose.

My dad's always complaining about Leonard, but last evening he stayed outside and talked to him for almost an hour. I think Leonard knows the right things to say.

WORKSHEET

A GOOD NEIGHBOR IS A QUIET NEIGHBOR

Sometimes it's cool to be quiet.

This guy up the street bought a Harley-Davidson motorcycle. When he rides it, he wears this black-leather outfit that makes him look like Zorro. But my mom and dad and the neighbors think he's a jerk because his bike makes too much noise.

Last Sunday morning, the guy started up his Harley and woke up the whole neighborhood, okay? Well, this did it. My dad and Mr. Barkley from next door went and had this talk with him. I guess he got pretty upset, because he threatened to sick his dog on them. So my dad called the police, and they came out and found out that he had this special muffler on his bike that made it sound extra loud. They told him to change it or else.

Now the bike is a lot quieter. And the guy looks just as cool in his black-leather Zorro outfit without all the noise. Which goes to show that you don't have to be loud to be cool. I mean . . . Zorro rode a horse.

WORKSHEET

A HAIR-RAISING STORY

Change is a natural thing.

For a long time, my dad's head seemed to be getting bigger. It was really a mystery to me. Weird. Maybe he was turning into an outer-space person, or something. Finally I asked my mom. I went, "Mom, how come Daddy's head is getting bigger?" She goes, "I don't know what you're talking about." I go, "Every time I look at Daddy, there seems to be a whole lot more to his head." Then she laughed and said, "Oh, I see what you mean. He's losing his hair."

I'd never ever thought about this before. I know that lots of stuff changes as people get older. Like they get wrinkles and all bent over and walk a lot slower and seem to be more grouchy. But hair? I never thought about it making your face look bigger.

When I mentioned this to my dad, he said it didn't bother him, but if it bugged me, he'd start wearing a hat. At least he hasn't lost his sense of humor.

WORKSHEET

BRRRRRRR

Change is often not what you think it's going to be.

Over Christmas we went to Vermont. The whole family. Because my mom wanted to see some snow. We live in Jacksonville, Florida, where it's warm and sunny. Snow? Forget it. So, anyway, we pack up the SUV and drive to Vermont, where we check into this bed and breakfast place that smelled like wet clothes. The man and woman who ran the place were real old and weird and talked funny and were so friendly they made you sick.

Well, we all sat around the place with nothing to do. There was only one TV, and it was downstairs in this big living room where most of the time people were watching the Home Shopping Network. And it snowed every day and was so cold we had to sleep in our sweaters. After three days, my mom couldn't take it anymore.

Next Christmas we're driving down to Miami.

WORKSHEET

_____

_____

_____

_____

_____

_____

_____

_____

_____

_____

_____

_____

SAD NEWS

Accepting bad news is part of growing up.

When I heard the phone ring in the middle of the night, I knew something was wrong. Telephone calls at this time are either wrong numbers or bad news. It was bad news. My grandmother had died.

At first, I didn't know what to do. I mean, I was sad and scared, and I couldn't get over the idea I'd never see my Grammy again. And my mom was super-upset and crying. It's bad enough for your grandmother to die, but your mother . . .

After a while we calmed down and all went down to the kitchen. Daddy fixed coffee and hot chocolate, and we sat around the kitchen table and talked. We talked for a long time. Till it started to get light outside. And I learned a lot. I learned a lot about families and how important they are. And for the first time I realized that someday I might get a bad phone call in the middle of the night, too.

WORKSHEET

_____

_____

_____

_____

_____

_____

_____

_____

_____

_____

_____

_____

NOT GUILTY

Unfairnness is part of life.

My parents bought me a computer, but I can't get near it because my pushy brother's always using it.

Last night, when I wanted to get on the Net, my stupid brother is looking up stuff for school. When I asked him how long he was going to be, he said, "Get lost, creep." I told him while he was looking up stuff he should look under "Jerk" for his picture. This makes him mad and he goes and throws a book at me, but I duck and it breaks a bedroom window.

When mom and dad come in to see what happened, he tells them that I got on his nerves. They jumped on me good. Like it's my fault the dummy throws a book through my window, right?

The way I look at it is, if you're little, you're gonna get the blame no matter what, because older people love to yell at little kids. And older people are supposed to be smarter, right? Well . . . they're not in my family. So far as I'm concerned, they should all be listed on the Internet at idiots.com.

WORKSHEET

_____

_____

_____

_____

_____

_____

_____

_____

_____

_____

_____

_____

BRAINIAC

It's nice to have smart friends.

My next-door neighbor is this real dorky kid who is different from everybody else. Her name is Mary Devers. She wears these really thick glasses and dresses weird. But she's super smart.

When my teacher asked if anyone knew the date of Andrew Jackson's birthday, Devers jumps up and rattles it off like it's nothing. Then she goes and names all the presidents–in order. She's like this big bunch of information walking around, you know. This is the reason she gets As in everything. Me? I have trouble remembering stuff. Even little things. Like yesterday. My mom asked me to go to the store and pick up a pint of cream and two cans of Chicken Feast cat food, okay? Well, when I get to the store, I can't remember what I'm supposed to get, so I come home with a pint of ice cream and two cans of chicken soup. I got yelled at good. Next time, I'm taking Devers along.

WORKSHEET

BE-BOP SHA-BANG

Music is in the ears of the beholder.

My parents listen to jazz all the time. I don't know what they see in it. It all sounds like someone took a bunch of music and threw it in a blender, or something.

Last week they made me go with them to this jazz concert in the park where people are sitting around eating and talking about jazz. The main thing I remember is that they said "man" a lot. And "like." For instance: "Like, man, this is really good food."

After about an hour, the band comes out. They're all wearing suits. Nobody on MTV wears *suits*. Then they all sit down behind these little stands and start making weird noises. My dad said that they were warming up. Then this main guy comes out and makes a speech. He said "man" and "like" a lot, too. Then he starts up the band. It sounded like our neighbor's Weed Whacker when it hits his drainpipe. After, when my parents asked me what I thought, I said, "Like, man, I thought it was awful."

WORKSHEET

_____

_____

_____

_____

_____

_____

_____

_____

_____

_____

_____

_____

SAY CHEESE

Lots of time we have to do stuff we don't wanna do.

Aw, c'mon, Mom. We had our picture taken last year. (*beat*) But I don't think anybody really cares if there's a picture of the family in our Christmas card or not. (*beat*) How do I know? Because I was over at Lawrence's one day when they got this picture from somebody. They trashed it right away. (*beat*) But Grandma must have a zillion pictures of us already. Besides, we see her every month. How much can we change? (*beat*) Aw, nuts! You mean we gotta go and get all dressed up and stand around while this dorky guy says, "Cheese"? Besides, his stuff isn't any good. In the last one, I looked mental and Dad's head looked like it was on crooked. I'll bet we got laughed at good for that one. Before people dumped it, that is. Nobody keeps 'em, Mom. If they do, how come when we go to the Berkeys, we never see the ones we send them? I'll tell you why: 'Cause the Berkeys feed 'em to their dog.

WORKSHEET

CHORES

Sometimes people try to get out of doing their share.

Look, Sue, I've only got two hands. Besides, how come I gotta do all the work around here while you sit around playing computer games? (*beat*) No you didn't. I cleaned up last time, remember? (*beat*) The bathrooms? You call that cleaning? All you did was pick up two towels and then go sit in front of the TV and eat a tube of Pringles. (*beat*) Tired? How can you be tired from picking up two towels? You're supposed to help out around here too, you know. (*beat*) No way! Mom never said that. She said we had to share. If you don't, I'm gonna let things go, and when Mom comes home, I'm gonna tell her what a goof-off you are. (*beat*) I will, too. I mean it. (*beat*) Good. That's more like it. (*beat*) What're you doing? That's no way to rinse a plate. (*beat*) You're what? You're only rinsing your half!

WORKSHEET

DIVORCE

Silence is not always golden.

I don't get to see my dad much since he and my mom got divorced. He moved to Phoenix a little over a year ago. I only go there twice a year. It's really awful.

Another thing that makes it bad is that my mom and dad don't speak to each other. They're still mad from stuff that happened a long time ago. So when I'm around my dad, I'm afraid to say anything good about my mom, and when I'm around my mom, I have to be careful not to say anything good about my dad. Which is hard because I like them both the same, even though they don't like each other.

Things used to be really neat when we were all together. Mom and dad seemed to like each other then. Then something happened. I don't understand it. All I know is that the way they act now sure doesn't make it easy for anyone.

WORKSHEET

EDUCATION

Parents want you to have the advantages they never had.

Maybe I won't wanna go to college, Dad. Maybe I'll be, like, like this person who figures out something important that will make me super rich. *(beat)* I know, but what about the man who started up Microsoft? I heard he never finished college. *(beat)* Yes, Bill Gates, that's his name. He's one of the richest people in the entire world. *(beat)* Well . . . maybe I'll turn out to be special, too. Who knows? Besides, everybody doesn't go to college, you know. You didn't, and you've done okay. *(beat)* You did? I didn't know that. You mean, you had to take care of your whole family? *(beat)* Wow! *(beat)* So you think college is really that important, huh? *(beat)* Well . . . in that case, I'll guess I'll go. I can wait a awhile to get rich.

WORKSHEET

COUNT YOUR BLESSINGS

You're seldom as bad off as you think.

My dad is, like, this magician, you know. Not for a living, just part time. And he's pretty good, too. He makes stuff disappear and money come out of your nose and turns doves into confetti. He goes around to schools and hospitals for nothing.

Yesterday I went with him to Mercy Hospital, where he did tricks for sick kids. He was a big hit and had them laughing and smiling. It was neat.

A lot of the kids were really sick, and some were crippled and in wheelchairs. I felt real bad for them. The thing I noticed most is that none of them complained. Not like most healthy kids I know, including me. I was all, "Why can't I have a new computer, and stuff" before I went. But now, now I figure it's not all that important. The more important thing is, I can walk.

WORKSHEET

FUN AND GAMES

You get rewarded for a job well done.

A bunch of us kids sold a bunch of magazines to raise money for school. I sold twenty. Mostly to my grandfather and grandmother and my Aunt Lilly. Mom and Dad bought six. I only sold one to our neighbors. One man slammed the door in my face. This is the reason I decided to sell them to my relatives over the phone. This way you don't have to walk so far.

As a reward for us selling so much, the school brought in these extreme games: a giant slide, a bungee thing, and this course you had to run through. My favorite, though, was the Velcro board. It was really cool. You wore these special jumpsuits that would stick to the board. I loved jumping as high as I could and sticking. When Heather Enos got stuck, it took two people to get her down. I guess this is what she gets for living on Snickers bars.

WORKSHEET

SAFETY FIRST

A car is not a kitchen or a phone booth.

Okay, but I still think eating in your car is gross. I mean, how come you can't wait till you get home or just stay and eat at Burger King, or wherever? (*beat*) C'mon, people can't be in that big a hurry.

Yesterday my dad and I saw this woman eating a whole meal in her SUV. (*beat*) No kidding. And she was using her steering wheel for a table. And she was weaving all over the freeway. My dad said there should be a law against eating while you're driving. He thinks the same thing about talking on cellphones, too.

When I told him your mom sometimes eats a hot dog when she drives us home from school, he said I couldn't ride with you guys anymore. (*beat*) Yep, he's gonna pick us up from now on. Maybe you'll wanna ride with us. This way you won't wind up at the hospital all covered with mustard.

WORKSHEET

_____

_____

_____

_____

_____

_____

_____

_____

_____

_____

_____

_____

BUSY, BUSY

When you try to do everything, you don't do much at all.

You see, it's like this: I'm on the soccer team and the volleyball team and I take tennis lessons and piano lessons. My sister is a Girl Scout, on the softball team, runs track, and just started doing gymnastics. My older brother plays baseball, football, soccer, and basketball, and is the drummer in a group called Music Modem. The whole bunch of us is doing something all the time. We never have time to see one another, or talk, or do much family stuff. When we're home, in between running around doing junk, we're always busy doing homework. My mom said she put 50,000 miles on our Jeep last year dragging us around. Sometimes I wonder if it's worth it. Sometimes I think we'd be more like a family if we all just stayed home and vegged out.

WORKSHEET

_____

_____

_____

_____

_____

_____

_____

_____

_____

_____

_____

_____

SILLY STUFF

Looks are not the most important thing.

If my mom's hair isn't just right, she goes nuts. It's like hair is the most important thing in the world. Like, I mean, what's hair? Hair isn't cool. Hair is hair. After I take a shower, I just dry it off and comb it and forget about it. But not my mom or my older sister or my aunts or my grandmothers. To them, hair is the biggest thing since the Internet. They talk about how you cut it and what color it should be and how long it should be and like that. Yesterday, I heard my mom telling my Aunt Sally that her hair was cute. How can hair be cute? Rabbits, maybe, kittens, but hair? Get real.

It seems like women are more hair-nutty than men. I never hear my dad or uncles talk about hair. My Uncle Ralph doesn't have any, and it doesn't seem to bother him. Although he does kinda look funny from the back; kinda like his shoulders are growing a grapefruit. But who cares? So what? Hair's no way as important as going to the mall.

WORKSHEET

LEFT OUT

New babies shouldn't get all the attention.

I know he's my brother, Mom. I know. But since you brought him home, all you and Dad do is mess with him. (*beat*) I know he's just a baby. But, I mean, do you have to be messing with him all the time? Before Danny came, we all used to do stuff together. Now, all we do is stay home because of Danny. (*beat*) Yeah, but for how long? I mean, he can't have attention forever. (*beat*) Yeah, I like him, too. He's real cute and makes nice noises and laughs funny. I think he's pretty cool. But I don't have to be hanging in his room messing with him all day long.

You think maybe this weekend we can go to a movie and hang out like we used to? And go shopping and stop by the park? (*beat*) But, gee, I mean . . . ya know, sometimes lately I feel like . . . I dunno . . . kinda . . . I dunno, it's kinda hard to explain. Sometimes I feel like I wish I was Danny.

WORKSHEET

CELL-MATES

Sometimes high-tech is pretty low.

We never go anyplace without cell phones. My whole family has them. My dad has his hooked on his belt like some dork robot. My sister has a bright red one that she whispers into like the whole world's a secret. My mom never takes hers out of her hand. My dad said he didn't know if we live after we die or not, so, just in case, he's gonna be buried with his.

I think cells are cool. I mean, you can get in touch with people, and they can get in touch with you almost anyplace. But, sometimes, cells are dumb. Like when you're out someplace eating and one of Mom's girlfriends calls and they talk about cute clothes all through your McNuggets. Or when you're at the Cineplex and your dad gets a business call right in the middle of cool special effects.

It used to be that we got calls on our answering machine and called back later. Now there's no more later, now there's just now. And I gotta feeling it's gonna get a whole lot worse: My mom just bought a Palm Pilot.

ORDER DIRECT

A WOMAN SPEAKS: WOMEN FAMOUS, INFAMOUS and UNKNOWN, ed. Cosentino. $12.95.

BETH HENLEY: MONOLOGUES for WOMEN, Henley. *Crimes of the Heart*, others. $9.95.

CITY WOMEN, Smith. $9.95.

CLASSIC MOUTH, ed. Cosentino. Speeches for kids from famous literature. $8.95.

COLD READING and HOW to BE GOOD at IT, Hoffman. $12.95.

DIALECT MONOLOGUES, Karshner/Stern. Book and cassette tape. $19.95.

DIALECT MONOLOGUES, VOL. II, Karshner/Stern. Book and cassette tape. $19.95.

DIALECT MONOLOGUES—CD VERSION, Karshner/Stern. $22.95.

FITTING IN. Monologues for kids, Mauro. $8.95.

FOR WOMEN: MONOLOGUES THEY HAVEN'T HEARD, Pomerance. $9.95.

FOR WOMEN: MORE MONOS THEY HAVEN'T HEARD, Pomerance. $9.95.

FOR WOMEN: POCKET MONOLOGUES from SHAKESPEARE, Dotterer. $9.95.

HIGH-SCHOOL MONOLOGUES THEY HAVEN'T HEARD, Karshner. $9.95.

KIDS' STUFF, Roddy. 30 great audition pieces for children. $9.95.

KNAVES, KNIGHTS, and KINGS, ed. Dotterer. Shakespeare's speeches for men. $8.95.

MINUTE MONOLOGUES for KIDS, Roddy. $9.95.

MODERN MONOLOGUES for MODERN KIDS, Mauro. $9.95.

MODERN SCENES for WOMEN, Pomerance. Scenes for today's actresses. $7.95.

MONOLOGUES for KIDS, Roddy. 28 wonderful speeches for boys and girls. $9.95.

MONOLOGUES for TEENAGE GIRLS, Pomerance. $9.95.

MONOLOGUES for TEENAGERS, Karshner. Contemporary teen speeches. $9.95.

MONOLOGUES for WOMEN, Pomerance. $9.95.

MONOLOGUES from CHEKHOV, trans. Cartwright. $8.95.

MONOLOGUES from GEORGE BERNARD SHAW, ed. Michaels. $7.95.

MONOLOGUES from MOLIERE, trans. Dotterer. $9.95.

MONOLOGUES from OSCAR WILDE, ed. Michaels. $7.95.

MONOLOGUES from the CLASSICS, ed. Karshner. $8.95.

MONOLOGUES THEY HAVEN'T HEARD, Karshner. Speeches for men and women. $9.95.

MORE MONOLOGUES HAVEN'T HEARD, Karshner. More living-language speeches. $9.95.

MORE MONOLOGUES for KIDS, Roddy. More great speeches for boys and girls. $9.95.

MORE MONOLOGUES for TEENAGERS, Karshner. $9.95.

NEIL SIMON MONOLOGUES, ed. Karshner. $14.95.

NEIL SIMON SCENES, ed. Karshner. $14.95.

POCKET MONOLOGUES for MEN, Karshner. $9.95.

POCKET MONOLOGUES for WOMEN, Pomerance. 30 modern speeches. $9.95.

POCKET MONOLOGUES: WORKING-CLASS CHARACTERS for WOMEN, Pomerance. $8.95.

RED LICORICE, Tippit. 31 great scene-monologues for preteens. $9.95.

SCENES for KIDS, Roddy. 30 scenes for girls and boys. $9.95.

SCENES for TEENAGERS, Karshner. Scenes for today's teen boys and girls. $9.95.

SHAKESPEARE'S LADIES, ed. Dotterer. $9.95.

SHAKESPEARE'S MONOLOGUES for WOMEN, ed. Dotterer. $9.95.

SHAKESPEARE'S MONOLOGUES THEY HAVEN'T HEARD, ed. Dotterer. $9.95.

TEENAGE MOUTH, Karshner. Modern monologues for young men and women. $9.95.

VOICES. Speeches from the writings of famous women, ed. Cosentino. $9.95.

WHEN KIDS ACHIEVE, Mauro. Positive monologues for preteen boys and girls. $8.95.

WOMAN, Pomerance. Monologues for actresses. $8.95.

YOU SAID a MOUTHFUL, Karshner. Tongue twisters galore. $8.95.

For details visit our on-line catalog at: dramaline.com